Toad in the Hole

A collection of recipes from The Greenbank Hotel Kitchen
Falmouth, Cornwall

Prosenjit Sanjay Kumar

Toad in the Hole

Copyright © 2010 Prosenjit Sanjay Kumar

All rights reserved

ISBN: 978-0-9565666-0-7

Published by Highway Church, Highway House, 2a Annear Road,

Kernick Business Park, Penryn, Cornwall TR10 9EW

Printed by R Booth Ltd, The Praze, Penryn Cornwall TR10 8AA

Table of Content:

Preface

Never has food and eating habits of human nature been more exciting than recent times. Many a splendid tale of extraordinary human feat is gracefully wrapped amongst the silent walls of the Greenbank Hotel in Falmouth, which once was the abode of Packet ship captains, and was where the famous words of "Wind in the willows" were hatched. When it comes to marrying the best of both the worlds, working as a Head chef of a historic, "Hotel by the river", life is like living a dream.

"Atithee Kutumbam"(Guest is god) is a Sanskrit scripture that was rooted deep into my early traditional Indian values. Carrying colorful vignettes from cooking experiences across Gargantuan Indian hotel kitchens, to royal Arabic mobile tents, landing work with Raymond Blanc was a perfect seasoning to my quest for learning how to cook from the heart.

Cornwall offers every opportunity to let your cooking imagination go wild. In the following anthology of recipes, I showcase some genuine and local Cornish Produce that talks for its own qualifications.

Each of these recipes have featured on our brasserie menus and have been widely enjoyed by discerning foodies. Try your hands on these magical combinations at home, and discover the joys of cooking.

Yours aye,

Prosenjit Sanjay Kumar

Prawns Peri peri, with honey brioche

This dish reminds me of my early cooking days in Goa. Sipping on cool bottles of beer, on a humid Indian summer day, prawns cooked in this fashion was a sensation only second to bliss. Enjoy the feeling of hot!

Ingredients to serve 2:
Preparation time: 15 minutes.
Marinade preparation:
12 prawns shelled and deveined
1 cup groundnut oil
10 fresh red chillies
1 large red onion, chopped finely
Juice of 4 fresh limes
1 bulb of garlic – shelled and chopped fine
1 cup fresh coriander – chopped
1 cup white wine vinegar
2 tablespoons Cornish sea salt
4 tablespoons sweet paprika

Method:
Mix the ingredients in a glass bowl – whisk for 2 minutes. Store, covered in the refrigerator for 24 hours to let the flavours release. Once aged, remove ¼ of the marinade and set aside to use as a dipping sauce.
Heat up a non stick pan.
Pour the groundnut oil in the pan, and place the prawns one by one, away from your body. Cook the prawns on one side and turn over after two minutes, until the tail turns bright orange. Pour in the marinade, and simmer the prawns for a couple of minutes. Serve hot with a lot of honey brioche, crunchy radish and red onion salad and tomato relish.
Sanjays Suggestion:
Marinate the prawns overnight, to pack in the flavours. This dish works really well with pancetta crisps.

Fresh and frozen prawns can be obtained from Matthew Stevens and sons at http://www.mstevensandson.co.uk/

Polgoon Peren steamed Fal Bay mussels, with chilli, ginger and coriander

My days in Cornwall began with identifying new produce and knowing unique producers. Kim and her unique cider was amongst the first, and I have never looked back...

Literally ready in minutes

Ingredients:
1 tablespoon vegetable oil
8 oz fresh mussels, bearded
4 oz. Polgoon vineyard Peren
3 tablespoon unsalted Cornish Butter
2 tablespoon fresh coriander leaves
1 large shallot, sliced
2 red chillies seeded and chopped finely
1 bulb ginger sliced thinly

Method:
Heat a large skillet to medium heat and add vegetable oil.
Add mussels and toss gently.
Add Peren, chillies and ginger; cover with a lid.
Discard any mussels that are not open.
Pour gently into large serving bowl garnish with some fresh coriander leaves and plenty of garlic bread.

Sanjay Says: Mussels and cider is a match made in heaven. This age old recipe works wonders with Peren's sharpness and marries well with the smoothness of chillies and ginger. Make sure you have plenty of bread to mop the sauce off the bowl.

For more information on Polgoon products log on to http://polgoonvineyard. vpweb.co.uk/default.html

Cornish new season asparagus, earlies and wild garlic Yarg veloute

In the circles of Cornwall's rich milk heritage, Cornish Yarg has already achieved the Hall of Fame. The deftness with which the ladies wrap nettle leaves around circular mounds of milk protein is an apple of any man's eyes.

Ingredients to serve 4:
Preparation time: 10 min
Cooking time: 5 min
1 large onion, chopped
4 teaspoons vegetable oil
3 tablespoons all-purpose flour
2 cups Cornish asparagus trimmed
2 cups semi skimmed milk
2 cups chicken stock
8 ounces Cornish earlies potato, cubed
1 wild garlic yarg sliced
⅓ cup sour cream

Method:
In a large saucepan cook onion in hot oil over medium heat until tender.
Sprinkle flour over onion and stir to coat.
Add chicken stock, asparagus, milk, and potatoes.
Cook and stir until thickened and bubbly; reduce heat.
Simmer, covered, for 10 to 12 minutes or until vegetables are tender, stirring occasionally.
Liquidize the soup using a hand blender.

If you want to know more about Cornish yarg cheeses, log on to http://www. lynherdairies.co.uk/index.html

Lamb shank Rogan Josh with crushed Bombay potatoes and mint yoghurt

Lamb is a staple part of an Indian diet. This dish reminds me of a typical winter Sunday afternoon when Mum would ceremoniously divide the aromatic bright red gravy between family members gathered around the dining table. The combination of tomato, subtle hints of spices in the crushed potatoes and the mildness of the mint yoghurt is a marriage made in heaven. Here at The Greenbank we recreate the age old recipe in our own special way.

Ingredients:
Preparation time: 40 minutes
Cooking time: 6 Hours
300g Natural Greek yoghurt
1 sprig mint (chopped)
200g new potatoes (boiled in their skin)
3g turmeric powder
1g chilli powder
2g ground coriander
1g ground ginger
2 liters lamb stock
4 whole cardamom pods
6 ripe plum tomatoes (chopped)
1 liter water
A pinch ground nutmeg
5g ground cumin
2 large onions (chopped roughly)
1 bunch fresh coriander leaves
4 large lamb shanks trimmed and tied with a twine
1 pinch saffron strand
25 ml vegetable oil

Method:

Pre heat the oven to 350f

Whisk a third of the yoghurt in a bowl, add a pinch of ground cumin and mix the chopped mint. Keep refrigerated.

Dust the lamb shanks with chilli powder, ground coriander, ginger and cumin.

Pour the vegetable oil in a roasting pan.

Place the lamb shanks in the pan and brown them carefully without splashing any hot oil.

Transfer the shanks to a plate and keep aside.

Brown the onion, add ¾ of the chopped tomatoes and soften them. Add the spices, saffron strands and yoghurt to the sauce and top it up with the lamb stock and water.

Return the lamb shanks to the pan, cover with a tin foil and cook in the pre heated oven . Cook for 6 hours so that the lamb falls off the bone.

For the Bombay crushed potatoes:

Heat some oil in a pan, cook off the ground cumin, and turmeric powder, add rest of the tomatoes. Add the boiled new potatoes and coat them generously with the spiced tomatoes. Crush the spiced potatoes and keep warm.

To serve.

Place a generous amount of the Bombay crushed potatoes in the centre of the plate. Spoon the tender lamb shank on top of the potatoes and ladle a generous spoonful of sauce around. Serve hot with some soothing mint yoghurt.

To source fresh local produce, and learn about West Country meats, log on to: http://www.etherington-meats.co.uk/

Garam Masala dusted Newlyn Bay fillet of Halibut served with crushed Bombay style Cornish earlies, new season Rowes Farm asparagus and coconut-curry butter

Masala fried fish is a definite part of the menu in any Bengali household in India. The unique flavour combinations, remind me of my Nan grating fresh coconut by her well seasoned hands, to prepare this delectable curry.

This fish dish is a great marriage between oriental flavours and fresh Cornish summer produce. Reminds me of a typical summer afternoon, discussing Sachin Tendulkars feats on the cricket pitch while enjoying a subtle South Indian fish dish in one of the eponymous Mumbai cafes, only inches away from the sea.

Ingredients to serve 4:
Preparation time: 15 min
Cooking time: 20 min
Ready in 35 min
180ml dry white wine
120ml heavy cream
80ml coconut milk
15g Greenbank curry powder
225g cold, unsalted butter, cut into pieces
Cornish sea salt to taste
60 ml vegetable oil
4 <150 Gms> fillets Newlyn Bay Halibut
15g garam masala

For the Bombay crushed earlies:
200g cornish earlies (boiled in their skin)
3g turmeric powder
1g chilli powder
2g ground coriander
1g ground ginger
1 bunch cornish asparagus trimmed.

Method:

For the sauce.

Pour white wine, cream, and coconut milk into a saucepan; season with curry powder. Bring to a light boil over medium-high heat, then reduce heat to medium-low, and simmer until the liquid has reduced to 1/2 cup (about 10 minutes).

When the liquid has reduced, turn heat to low and whisk in the butter, a few cubes at a time, until all of the butter has incorporated. Do not allow the mixture to boil or else it will separate. When the butter has incorporated, season to taste with salt and set aside to keep warm.

Heat the oil in a sauté pan over medium-high heat until it begins to smoke. While the oil is heating, lightly season both sides of the Halibut with garam masala and salt.

Sear the Halibut in the hot oil for 3 to 4 minutes on one side, then turn over, and continue cooking for 2 to 3 minutes until done. Deglaze with clarified butter and finish with a drizzle with a squeeze of lemon. Briefly drain on paper towels to absorb excess oil, keep aside.

For the Bombay crushed potatoes.

Heat some oil in a pan, cook off the ground cumin and turmeric powder and add the rest of the tomatoes.

Add the boiled cornish earlies and coat them generously with the spiced tomatoes.

Crush the spiced potatoes and keep warm.

Blanch the cornish asparagus spears in salted water for 2-3 minutes and keep aside.

To serve.

Spoon a generous amount of crushed earlies on the fish plate.

Sit the Halibut on top, and place the blanched asparagus spears criss-crossing each other.

Drizzle the coconut butter around and garnish with a bunch of Confit cherry tomatoes on the vine, and a pickled lemon wedge.

Fresh local vegetables are delivered daily to us by, http://www.hendys.net/

Chickpea, spinach and butternut squash curry - with cumin pea pilaf and pineapple raita

The unique combination of chickpeas and butternut squash is a definite part of the menu in any Bengali house-hold in India. Brings back sweet memory scents of my Nan carving fresh pumpkins with a cleaver, while her umpteen young grandchildren huddled around the roaring kiln on a chilly December afternoon.

Ingredients to serve 4:
1 onion finely chopped
200g baby spinach leaves, washed and excess water squeezed out
2 cloves garlic, finely chopped
1 butternut squash, 6-8 inches high, peeled and diced with seeds scooped out
100gms cooked chickpeas
1 fresh tomato
1 tin coconut milk
1 green chilli, finely chopped
20g ginger, peeled and finely chopped
A handful of chopped fresh coriander
Half a lemon

Spices:
1 tbsp cumin seed
1 tbsp coriander seed
½ tbsp turmeric
8g garam masala powder

Method:
Grind the spices in a food processor (more traditionally in a mortar).
Fry the onion until translucent over a medium heat in some vegetable oil.
Add the garlic, ginger and chilli for a minute or so.
Add the spices for a minute or so- you'll start to smell them as they temper.
Add the butternut squash and coat in the ingredients in the pan.

Cook for a couple of minutes.
Add the tomatoes and coconut milk, and cook for 10-15 minutes until the squash is cooked.
Drain the chickpeas and add to the sauce.
Also add the spinach.
When the spinach is wilted and the chickpeas are warmed through, add the coriander and a squeeze of lemon juice.
Season to taste. Serve hot with some cumin pea pilaf and pineapple raita

We source our dairy products daily from, http://www.lilliebrothers.co.uk/

Emily's apple crumble cake with cinnamon yoghurt

Apple crumble, although the most humble of English desserts, is a special revelation when cooked right. Here is our very own pastry chef Emily's version of an age old simple classic.

Ingredients to serve 8:
Cooking time: 1 hour
Oven: 180 degrees
Topping:
25 g unsalted butter
75 g self raising flour
25g caster sugar
1 tablespoon water
Base:
50g softened butter
50g caster sugar
1 egg beaten
2 drops vanilla essence
100g self raising flour
2 cooking apples peeled cored

Method:
Grease a 20 cm cake tin with butter and place a butter paper on it.
For the topping:
Rub the butter into flour and stir in the sugar. Sprinkle the water and mix into a little dough. Keep aside
For the base:
Cream the butter and sugar together until light and fluffy. Beat in the egg and vanilla essence and finally stir in the flour.
Spread at the bottom of the lined cake tin. Arrange the cooking apple slices on top and cover completely with crumble topping.
Bake in a pre heated oven for one hour and cool down slightly before turning out.
To serve:
Serve a delicious wedge of the apple crumble cake with cinnamon yoghurt and Cornish clotted cream.

Roddas Jam roly poly

This dessert reminds me of an early Kentish summer afternoon, with my pastry chef hunting for ideas while rummaging through the pages of Larousse Gastronomique,and repeating often enough," How can we use British produce to imitate a French dessert", e voila...

(A roly-poly is a traditional British dessert similar to an American jelly roll. In this version, the scone-like pastry is spread with tangy sweet raspberry and rhubarb jam, and then baked.)

Ingredients to serve 6:
Filling:
½ pound fresh rhubarb, cut crosswise into ½-inch-thick slices
½ cup sugar
1 tablespoon water
½ cup raspberry jam
Dough:
2 cups all purpose flour
2 tablespoons sugar
2 teaspoons baking powder
½ teaspoon salt
10 tablespoons frozen unsalted butter
⅔ cup (or more) ice water
1 tablespoon whipping cream beaten with 1 tablespoon sugar (for glaze)

Method:
For filling:
Combine rhubarb, sugar, and 1 tablespoon of water in a medium sauce-pan. Stir over medium heat until sugar dissolves. Cover and cook until rhubarb softens to a thick pulp, stirring often (about 8 minutes). Mix in jam. Cool.
Do ahead (Can be made 1 week ahead).
Cover and chill.

For dough:

Sift flour; sugar; baking powder and salt into a large bowl.

Using large holes on a box grater, grate frozen butter into a bowl, then stir to blend.

Cover and freeze at least 15 minutes.

Preheat oven to 400°F.

Line large rimmed baking sheet with parchment paper.

Add ⅔ cup of ice water to flour mixture, tossing until soft dough forms, adding more ice water by tablespoonfuls if dough is stiff.

Transfer to lightly floured surface; knead gently 5 or 6 turns (butter should remain in firm pieces).

Roll out dough to 12x9 inch rectangle.

Spread 6 tablespoons filling over dough, leaving 1-inch plain border on all sides.

Starting at 1 long side, roll up jelly-roll style and seal seam.

Place seam side down on prepared sheet.

Seal ends.

Brush glaze over pastry.

Bake pastry until golden (jam may leak out), about 30 minutes. Cool pastry briefly.

Cornwall and clotted cream, work hand in hand, and is procured locally from, http://www.roddas.co.uk/

Saffron, pistachio and cardamom kulfi

Kulfi or Qulfi is a popular flavored frozen dessert made from milk which originated in South Asia and is popular throughout neighboring countries in the Middle East.

Unlike other ice cream, kulfi takes a very long time to melt. It comes in various flavors, including pistachio; rose; mango; cardamom (elaichi) and saffron.

Ingredients to serve 1:
1 ½ cup whole milk
1 ½ cup condensed milk
4 whole cardamom pods
3g saffron threads
5 tbs caster Sugar
⅛ cup chopped pistachios

Method:
Pour the whole milk and condensed milk into your pan and add the cardamom pods.
Heat on medium flame.
Once the milk is warm, take 2 tablespoons of milk and soak the saffron for a few minutes, then pour the saffron infused milk back into the pan.
Stir the liquid often while it all cooks down to ⅓ of the liquid.
Then strain out the cardamom pods, add the sugar and pistachios and cook for a few more minutes.
Churn the rich saffron cream for a couple of minutes.
Pour into molds and freeze until solid.

All our ice creams come from local, organic farmhouse, http://www.roskillys. co.uk/

In acknowledgement

Good things in life happen to people who dare to dream. Greenbank Hotel and my journey into the world of writing would never have been successful without the support of Kearan, my General Manager. Taking a gamble on me, and sticking to his decision right through the ups and downs of kitchen life, he has been both supportive and an ideal manager. I will never forget the day when Kearan drove me to my first cooking demonstration, in a rented van, with sauce running all over the carpet.

A notable amount of support arises from my suppliers, who work day and night to procure the best of the best produce from in and around Cornwall.

Creating a work life balance is always a pirouettes job when it comes to being a chef. Thanks to the patience of Shilpa, my childhood friend and wife, umpteen cups of milk laced hot chocolates and good inspirational food has never been an issue.

A considerable amount of credit also goes to each one of you, who reads my books, recipes and vignettes and supports various charitable organiasations in return, thus making the world we live in, a much more amicable place to cohabit.

Happy cooking.

Further reading

On behalf of my team at the Greenbank Hotel, I am hopeful that this anthology of recipes has excited your nerves, and made you respect food in a unique way.

Cooking never stops here!

So, what are you waiting for: discover new flavours, learn new tricks, entertain and be entertained by the Joys of Cooking.

And, above all,

Never give up!!!

For further recipe ideas and updates, log on to: http://www.scribd.com/ Prosenjit76

Measurements (British, metric and US)

* 1 ounce flour = 25g = quarter cup
* 4 ounces flour = 125g = 1 cup
* 8 ounces flour = 250g = 2 cups
* 2 ounces breadcrumbs (fresh) = 60g = 1 cup
* 4 ounces breadcrumbs (dry) = 125g = 1 cup
* 4 ounces oatmeal = 125g = 1 cup (scant)
* 5 ounces currants = 150g = 1 cup
* 4 ounces shredded suet = 125g = 1 cup (scant)
* 4 ounces butter and other fats, including cheese = 125g = 1stick
* 8 ounces butter and other fats, including grated cheese = 250g = 1 cup
* 7 ounces caster/granulated sugar = 200g = 1 cup
* 8 ounces caster/granulated sugar = 250g = 1 and a quarter cups
* 8 ounces meat (chopped/minced/ground) = 250g = 1 cup
* 8 ounces cooked, mashed potatoes = 250g =1 cup
* 1 ounce (1oz) = 1 rounded tablespoon
* 1 tablespoon of liquid = 3 teaspoons
* 1 teaspoon liquid = 5ml
* 1 British teaspoon is the same as an American teaspoon
* 1 British tablespoon liquid = 17.7ml
* 1 US tablespoon liquid =14.2ml
* 8 tablespoons = 4 fluid ounces = 125ml = Half cup
* 8 fluid ounces = 250ml = 1 cup (Half a US pint)
* half pint/10 fluid ounces = 300ml = 1 and a quarter cups (scant)
* 3 quarters of a pint/15 fluid ounces = 450 ml =2 cups (scant) or 1 US pint
* 1 British pint/20 fluid ounces = 600ml = 2 and a half cups

Oven Temperatures
* Gas Mark 1 = 275°F = 140°C
* Gas Mark 2 = 300°F = 150°C
* Gas Mark 3 = 325°F = 170°C
* Gas Mark 4 = 355°F = 180°C
* Gas Mark 5 = 375°F = 190°C
* Gas Mark 6 = 400°F = 200°C
* Gas Mark 7 = 425°F = 220°C
* Gas Mark 8 = 455°F = 230°C

History of the Greenbank Hotel

Dating from 1640 the Greenbank is Falmouth's oldest hotel and is a fascinating collection of sympathetically and beautifully restored buildings perched on the sea wall and private quay. Falmouth itself lies at the mouth of the world's third largest natural harbour and the Fal estuary's sheltered anchorage has been of strategic importance to the defence of Britain since Tudor times. Henry VIII built the twin castles of Pendennis and St Mawes to protect this anchorage.

The sea has always played a part in the history of the Greenbank Hotel. In 1688, the Post Office chose Falmouth as its principal port for handling mail and for the next 162 years the Falmouth Packets, fast and lightly armed against attack, sailed on regular schedules with mail, passengers and important cargo. Throughout this period the great Sea Captains of the day kept lodgings here whilst in the 1930's the hotel hosted the owners of the J class yachts as they raced the waters of the Fal.

The Greenbank Hotel has had its share of famous visitors. Kenneth Grahame's classic "Wind in the Willows" began as a series of letters sent to his son. The first two were written at the Greenbank Hotel while Grahame was a guest in May 1907. Reproductions of the letters are on display in the hotel along with Florence Nightingale's entry in the register.

We often wonder how many souls have spent their last night on home soil here before descending the sweeping staircase and embarking on adventures and new lives in foreign lands? This is a place with many a story to tell. Nightlife and wildlife, landscape and seascape, history and mystery – Falmouth hotels don't get much better than this.

www.greenbank-hotel.co.uk

King's Chef swaps Saudi palace for Falmouth hotel

The former Chef to the King of Saudi Arabia now finds himself catering for a very different set of customers.

Sanjay Kumar, 32, worked as Chef in Charge to HRH King Fahad at the Al Riyadh Palace for over two years. Now he is control of the kitchen at Falmouth's oldest hotel, the Greenbank and has unveiled his new menu.

Sanjay left the royal kitchen in 2003, to work under world-famous Michelin-starred chef Raymond Blanc at his Le Petit Blanc restaurants in both Oxford and Manchester, and featured in the TV series A Day in the Life of Raymond Blanc. He has also worked at the multiple award-winning Hotel du Vin in Tunbridge Wells.

"I've had some wonderful experiences through cooking," says Indian-born Sanjay. "It has given me the opportunity to travel the world, meet all kinds of people, and, of course, to discover new flavours, ingredients and techniques.

"Whether you're preparing a royal banquet, or cooking for the maestro, Monsieur Blanc himself, the pressure is always on to deliver really great food. I'm looking forward to maintaining that kind of standard using Cornwall's wonderful local produce."

True to his word, Sanjay's new summer menu, his first at the Greenbank, is notable for its imaginative use of Cornish ingredients.

"I mainly cook modern English and classical French cuisine, but it was going with my father to traditional river fish markets in India, and the way my mother transformed those local ingredients into wonderful dishes, that fired my imagination and really made me want to be a Chef – and that passion has always remained," he said.

"Even today, my vision is to support our hardworking local farmers, fishermen and butchers, and to help introduce a new generation of Chefs to the same joys of cooking. I couldn't ask for a more beautiful setting to achieve that than the Greenbank, and I'm delighted to be here."

My food in my words

Born into a traditional Indian family, food was always the focal point of my life.

I was enthralled by the frequent trips to the local fish market with my father to see fresh river water fish being gutted . A fascination about the chemistry of cooking and how my mother could turn ordinary meat and vegetables into delectable curries, drew me into being a chef for the rest of my life.

After working in various parts of India and Saudi Arabia, I got the unique chance to be a part of the Raymond Blanc kitchens in Oxford. Food had never been such an enlightening experience than being trained under the deft eyes of Monsieur Blanc himself. While French classical food was the base, the training instilled in me the concept of modern English food using fresh, seasonal local produce.

To further my quest towards my hunger to learn more about the marriage of fine food and wine, my next stop was Hotel Du Vin, Tunbridge wells. Working for Hotel Du Vin, gave me an opportunity to discover food in the perspective of a meal complemented with wine and cigars, while being trained in various managerial disciplines from people development to cost control .

My next step in the wonderful journey of cooking is Greenbank Hotel, Falmouth . With a vast coastline, and a unique landscape, Cornwall has a great potential to offer. Nothing can compare to having a bowl of steamed mussels with a glass of chardonnay, knowing that the fish has just been plucked a few moments ago out of the water meters away. My role here in the Greenbank Hotel is to produce a sustainable organic and nature friendly menu, by sourcing produce meticulously farmed by hard working fishermen, farmers and butchers of the region while training the chefs of the next generation to enjoy the joys of cooking.